The Parish System

The same yesterday, today and for ever?

Mark Burkill

The Latimer Trust

The Parish System
The same yesterday, today and forever?

© 2005 by Mark Burkill
ISBN 0 946307 52 0

Published by the Latimer Trust
PO Box 26685
London N14 4XQ

www.latimertrust.org

CONTENTS

1. Introduction   1

2. The Origins of the Parish System   6

3. The Gathering Storm:
   The Growing Inadequacies of the Parish System   25

4. The Parish System and Anglicanism   41

5. The Parish System and Mission Today   52

Bibliography   62

Chapter One:
Introduction

What is normally known as 'the parish system' is intimately associated with the structure and organisation of the Church of England. At its best it has noble ideals of evangelising the nation and providing pastoral care for all. Yet its practical expression today frequently frustrates the ministry of many Christians, particularly where there is an overriding concern with maintaining the *status quo* and an unthinking adherence to boundaries and geographical territoriality.

Long ago JC Ryle warned about the dangers of the parish system an idol[1] and there are numerous current expressions of the frustrations that many have with its practical expression in the twenty-first century. These criticisms come from a variety of theological perspectives. Thus Edward Norman, who has a high-church background, speaks about today as a "time when the parish system is proving to be wholly inadequate to meet modern social needs, and when it is anyway simultaneously collapsing under financial constraints."[2] Anthea Jones, despite her love for the parish and its history evident in *A Thousand Years of the English Parish*, can say "It has become imperative to rethink the parish."[3] Nick Spencer, an evangelical seeking to present a way forward for the parish system today, feels moved to say

---

[1] J.C. Ryle, *Can They be Brought in?* (Hunt & Co.: London: 1883), p 28.
[2] E.R. Norman, *Anglican Difficulties: A New Syllabus of Errors* (Morehouse, London: 2004), p 5. Norman also speaks of "antiquated parochial units" (p 143).
[3] A. Jones, *A Thousand Years of the English Parish: Medieval Patterns and Modern Interpretations* (Windrush Press, Moreton-in-Marsh: 2000), p 298.

that "the parish system was not brought down from Mount Sinai pure and divinely inspired, but evolved and adapted to suit the needs of English worshippers. In spite of what many non-Christians think, the parish is not set in stone".[4] John Tiller agrees in his foreword to the book *New Wineskins*: "The Church of England has got to be flexible enough to embrace and encourage these alternatives to the parochial system if it is going to have any kind of significant place in the future spiritual life of our nation".[5] The obstacles that the parish system can place in the way of effective mission has created such concern that even an official Church of England report, entitled *Mission-shaped Church,* recognises that the "existing parochial system alone is no longer able fully to deliver its underlying mission purpose".[6]

The purpose of this study is to understand the origins of what is termed the parish system and to explore its association with Anglicanism. It aims also to demonstrate that the parish system is ineffective and incapable of delivering what it claims in many areas, and that this is not merely because of social change. The study highlights how many seek to turn a blind eye to the way that the growth of

---

[4] N. Spencer, *Parochial Vision: The Future of the English Parish* (Paternoster, Carlisle: 2004), p xv.
[5] D. Pytches and B. Skinner, *New Wineskins: A Plea for Radical Rethinking in the Church of England to Enable Normal Church Growth to Take Effect Beyond Existing Parish Boundaries* (Eagle, Guildford: 1991) p xii.
[6] G.Cray, *Mission-shaped Church: Church Planting and Fresh Expressions of Church in a Changing Context* (Church House Publishing, London: 2004) p xi. This is further reinforced by a recent report to the Archbishops' Council chaired by Professor Peter Toyne. See, for example, paragraph 1.02 in P. Toyne, *A Measure for Measures: In Mission and Ministry* (Church House Publishing, London: 2004) p 1.

theological diversity has rendered the system meaningless in a number of respects. Finally ways in which the best ideals of the parish system may be expressed in Christian mission today are explored.

The key thing to bear in mind in discussing the merits of the parish system and its application today is that it is a structural and organisational feature of English Christianity and as such it should serve Christian mission rather than hinder that work. This is indeed how pastoral care was understood before the Norman conquest, long before the current parochial system appeared: "What unites them [the early medieval churches] is not a specific set of pastoral duties but their approach to achieving their theological aims. Organization is of secondary importance".[7] That was the conviction of those who were involved in Christian ministry in the earliest centuries of the Church's presence in England.

In regarding the parish system as very much a secondary feature of English Christianity we are doing no more than following the priorities of the New Testament. The progress of the Christian community at Ephesus illustrates this. Early developments at Ephesus, including the apostle Paul's lengthy period of ministry there, are described in Acts 18-20. We know that elders were appointed to lead and rule the church at Ephesus from the reference to Paul summoning them a little while afterwards to meet him at Miletus (Acts 20:17). This appointment of elders was of course Paul's general practice in towns he evangelised (cf. Acts 14:23; Titus 1:5). As Paul gives his farewell address to the Ephesian elders in Acts 20 his priorities are very

---

[7] J. Blair and R. Sharpe, 'Introduction' in J. Blair and R. Sharpe (eds), *Pastoral Care before the Parish* (Leicester University Press, Leicester: 1992) pp 1-10, p 1.

instructive. He does not envisage the health of the Christian community as being guaranteed by a particular form of organisation (though his conviction that order is necessary is plain from his appointment of the elders). His chief concern for the future is rather safeguarding against false teaching through a ministry which follows his own example of proclaiming the whole will of God. Therefore he does not commit the Ephesian Christians and their leaders to a proper organisational structure or to a nascent parish system, but to God and the word of his grace (Acts 20:32). The subsequent letter Paul wrote to Ephesus reveals a variety of ministries using different gifts, but the growing up into Christ is achieved through "speaking the truth in love" rather than the establishment of a particular structure for the exercise of these ministries (Eph 4:7-16). A similar sense of priorities is revealed when Paul writes the pastoral letters to Timothy who is working in Ephesus. Once again it is the concern for true teaching that pervades the correspondence, even though the need for order is affirmed. Timothy is reminded of the qualities appropriate for elders and urged to watch his own life and doctrine closely (1 Tim 3:1-7; 4:16). Paul does not envisage the Ephesian church being kept from wandering away from the faith (1 Tim 6:21) simply by the existence of elders and organisational structures, but through the sound doctrine that those elders must teach. The final glimpse of the Ephesian church in the New Testament is found in Rev 2:1-7. On this occasion the Ephesian Christians are strongly rebuked and warned about the loss of their first love. Nevertheless they are commended for being discerning about false teaching, apparently expressed in the practices of the Nicolaitans. In these circumstances the continued existence of the church in Ephesus (symbolised by the lampstand in

2:5) can only be ensured by the Christians' repenting and doing the things which they did at first. Once again the form of church organisation is not the chief priority. Teaching the truth was the greatest priority for the healthy growing churches of the apostolic age. If local churches are to engage in effective mission today then the parish system must be recognised as a secondary feature of English Christianity which must be adapted where necessary to the greater priority of enabling the people of England to hear the Christian message and to build their lives upon it.

Chapter Two:
The Origins of the Parish System

It is not usually appreciated that the Christian Church existed in England for many centuries prior to the definitive establishment of the parish system. Most observers place that establishment as taking place by the twelfth century. Thus George Addleshaw, in viewing the European picture as a whole, states: "By mid 12th century the dioceses of Europe had largely been broken up into units. Each of these units had its own church and priest and endowment. It was called a parish, a name in the early days of the Church reserved for what we call today a diocese".[8]

Two more recent authoritative studies confirm this. Norman Pounds in his *History of the English Parish* says "A system of parishes had begun to evolve during the middle Anglo/Saxon period and by the end of the twelfth century it had been extended over most of the country."[9] Similarly Jones, in her *A Thousand Years of the English Parish,* speaks of the term 'parish' in these terms: "The word parish implied two things: spiritual care of a group of people, and a territory with definite boundaries. The territorial pattern of English parishes emerged gradually and was substantially in place by the end of the twelfth century."[10]

---

[8] G.W.O. Addleshaw, *The Early Parochial System and the Divine Office* (A.R. Mowbray for the Alcuin Club, London: 1957) p 5.
[9] N.J.G. Pounds, *A History of the English Parish* (Cambridge University Press, Cambridge: 2000) p 3.
[10] Jones, *A Thousand Years of the English Parish*, p 15.

We must particularly note that it was issue of the tithes which made parish boundaries a matter of such importance at this period. Jones points out that "Gratian's collection of church canons about 1140, the Decretum, reinforced their territorial rather than their pastoral aspect; he helped establish that tithes should be paid to the church within whose parish the land was situated".[11] She remarks how this had the effect of refining the concept of a parish:

> "The bishops' policy in their councils was to protect the rights of older churches and to resist any increase in lay power. It was established that only one parish church could have responsibility for the cure of souls of a group of inhabitants; 'within one boundary there are not to be many baptismal churches, but one, with a number of chapels', and that the parish church should have a permanent endowment of glebeland, tithes, and offerings which constituted the 'title' of that church. Burial rights, baptismal rights and tithes became the 'normal definition' of a parish church. This meant that 'strict parochial boundaries of the kind familiar to us today can never have existed before the twelfth century.'"[12]

Pounds also remarks on the elaboration of canon law that was taking place at this time and how tithe differed from other financial burdens in being territorial rather than personal.[13] Significantly, Jones can then refer to the result of these developments as being a "freezing of the pattern of parishes" at this point in time.[14]

If we are going to assess the appropriate role the parish system should have today then we need to understand both its origins and development. Furthermore we will also

---

[11] Jones, *A Thousand Years of the English Parish*, p 49.
[12] Jones, *A Thousand Years of the English Parish*, p 49, also using material from C.N.L. Brooke and P.H. Hase (referenced on p 312).
[13] Pounds, *A History of the English Parish*, pp 41, 46.
[14] Jones, *A Thousand Years of the English Parish*, pp 49, 121.

need to appreciate the variety of ways in which pastoral care and mission was undertaken both before and after this 'freezing' of the pattern of parishes. It therefore makes sense to look at the development of pastoral care and mission prior to the twelfth century and then to look at the system from that period onwards.

Pastoral care and mission before the twelfth century

Christianity arrived in England during the Roman period. Although there is only limited evidence available at this time it is possible for William Frend to say that Christianity in Roman Britain showed the same urban episcopal organisation as the older churches in the west.[15] Nevertheless by the time of Augustine's arrival in England in 597 that organisation had disappeared.

Frend sees the work of Martin of Tours as vital. In Gaul during the late fourth century Martin carried out a ruthless anti-pagan mission in those areas outside the towns where Christianity had hardly penetrated, and then "He established a rudimentary parish system to consolidate his work of evangelisation".[16] Others elsewhere imitated his work but crucially this did not really happen in Britain. If there had been another 50 years of the *Pax Romana* in Britain then an effective parish system might have been established; however this did not take place. Thus Frend sees the period 430-450 as witnessing the practical destruction of episcopally-based

---

[15] W.H.C. Frend, 'Romano-British Christianity and the West: Comparisons and Contrasts', in S.M. Pearce (ed.) *The Early Church in W. Britain and Ireland: Studies Presented to C.A. Ralegh Radford, Arising from a Conference Organised in his Honour by the Devon Archaeological Society and Exeter City Museum* (B.A.R., Oxford: 1982) pp 5-16, p 5.
[16] Frend, *Romano-British Christianity and the West*, p 9.

Christianity in Britain. Pounds agrees with this picture, at least as far as Christianity in lowland Britain was concerned. He states that in Britain "both cities and bishoprics lapsed at some date in the fifth century, and the invading Anglo-Saxons probably found little more than their ruins."[17]

In understanding the development of pastoral care in England before the freezing of the parish system in the twelfth century it is easy for the picture to be dominated by the outworking of Gregory I's mission to the Anglo-Saxons from 597 onwards. This is partly because Bede's *Ecclesiastical History of the English People* is such an important source of information at this period. Yet Jones points out that the very focus of Augustine's mission on the recently arrived Anglo-Saxons suggests that there was already a British church (i.e. among the earlier indigenous people).[18] While Bede accuses the British of failing to evangelise the invading Anglo-Saxons, the British were of course still present in considerable areas of what we know as England today. Later we will see the significance of this for the parish system.

On the arrival of Augustine there were at least seven Anglo-Saxon kingdoms[19] with rather unstable boundaries. Although the instructions which Gregory I gave to Augustine for organising the church were in line with his experience in Italy, the fact was that those structures had to accommodate the political realities that existed in England.[20] Thus: "Anglo-Saxon kingdoms were the first parishes, each under the care

[17] Pounds, *A History of the English Parish*, p 12.
[18] Jones, *A Thousand Years of the English Parish*, p 29.
[19] Jones, *A Thousand Years of the English Parish*, pp 29-30.
[20] See Pounds, *A History of the English Parish*, p 17 for a list of the kingdoms and their corresponding dioceses.

of a bishop."[21] It is from this state of affairs that we find the anachronistic modern contention that the diocese is the parish or that the diocese is the key unit of church life.[22] By the end of the seventh century, Christianity was the dominant religion in England. It was initially a religion imposed from above through the conversion of the kings.

In the period that followed, dioceses were subdivided as certain kingdoms grew and were then subdivided for administrative purposes. Wessex for example was divided into shires, possibly even before 700. These subdivisions formed the basis for new dioceses in the tenth century.[23] In this period we need to see how churches came to be founded if we are to understand how Christianity was consolidated and pastoral care provided. Jones identifies three sources for the foundation of major churches in the late seventh century.[24] First, kings were important. They worked with 'their' bishops to provide churches, not so much for their kingdom as a whole, but for their centres of administration -

---

[21] Jones, *A Thousand Years of the English Parish*, p 30.
[22] To make such assertions shows no appreciation of the way in which the realities these terms expressed changed as Christianity took root in England and elsewhere. Addleshaw *The Early Parochial System and the Divine Office* p 5 reminds us that parish used to be the term used for what we now call a diocese. A modern expression of this confusion between parish and diocese is seen for example in the ARCIC *Final Report* (CTS/SPCK, London, 1982) p 55 III Authority in the Communion of the Churches, paragraph 8: "The unity of local communities under one bishop constitutes what is commonly meant in our two communions by 'a local church'". Note also how Paul Avis can state that in Anglicanism the diocese is regarded as the local church (P. Avis, *The Anglican Understanding of the Church: An Introduction* (SPCK, London: 2000) p 64). This is more cautiously asserted by Malcolm Brown in Toyne, *A Measure for Measures*, p 115.
[23] Jones, *A Thousand Years of the English Parish*, p 35.
[24] Jones, *A Thousand Years of the English Parish*, pp 39-40.

the royal vills. Thus it can be argued that the minster place-names in Dorset indicate a group of major churches founded under King Ine who ruled from 688-726. Landowners formed a second group responsible for the foundation of major churches at this period. The third impetus for the provision of key churches came from those who founded monasteries which they ruled personally.

The word minster is usually employed to describe all these major church foundations. This Anglo-Saxon word is derived from the Latin *monasterium* which also naturally gave rise to the later English term 'monastery'. However one needs to be very cautious in using any of these terms. It is all too easy to read particular anachronistic ideas and concepts of organisation into the use of them. For example the word 'monastery' in modern usage has acquired the connotation of contemplative regularity and of Benedictinism, yet this (of course) is thoroughly inappropriate for the Anglo-Saxon period.[25] It is preferable to note Alan Thacker's comment that *monasterium* and the English 'minster' embraced communities of very different size, and status, and ways of life.[26] Pounds is also alert to this and quotes Christopher Brooke's warning that 'minster' is a concept of marvellous ambiguity.[27] Pounds therefore properly concludes that "The Anglo-Saxon minster was essentially a centre for missionary activity."[28] This reminds us that the primary purpose of these

---

[25] S. Foot, 'Anglo-Saxon Minsters: A Review of Terminology', in J. Blair and R. Sharpe (eds), *Pastoral Care before the Parish*, pp 212-225, p 215.
[26] A. Thacker, 'Monks, Preaching and Pastoral Care in Early Anglo-Saxon England', in J. Blair and R. Sharpe (eds), *Pastoral Care before the Parish*, pp 137-170, p 139.
[27] Pounds, *A History of the English Parish*, p 17.
[28] Pounds, *A History of the English Parish*, p 18.

major churches was Christian mission and its consolidation through pastoral care, while indicating that the way in which this was done was enormously varied.

The relevance of this overview for a study of the parish system is that the minster's field of activity would be called its *parochia*, the Latin term normally translated parish. However at this stage it must be stressed that *parochia* was a term which was linked to the activity of Christian ministry. Although it inevitably had some territorial connotations that came from the travelling distance which was reasonably possible from the minster, it certainly did not have the rigid boundaries that we tend to associate with the word today. One can therefore readily see the attraction that the historical reality of the minster model of ministry holds for many in the Church of England today, since it stresses outreach through ministerial teams in a variety of forms. Such a manner of operation provides a vision for an alternative to the parish system in reaching England today.[29] Nevertheless one must be cautious in speaking of *the* minster model because its attractive variety in form came from personal initiative rather than the imposition of a systematised form of outreach.[30] Furthermore we must recall that the Anglo-Saxon minster operated in a rural setting which is vastly different from that which is generally found in Christian ministry in most Western nations today.

---

[29] Spencer, *Parochial Vision*, p xv.
[30] Pounds, *A History of the English Parish,* pp 21-22 emphasises that the danger in using the word 'system' is that it implies minsters were comparable in extent and in the nature of their functions. The reality was much more complex and minsters varied enormously according to the patronage they had received and the extent of the area dependent upon them.

The prevalence of minsters with their accompanying *parochiae* in circumscribing Christian pastoral activity in Anglo-Saxon England has led to the 'minster hypothesis' as a way of describing how pastoral care developed in the centuries that followed the foundation of these churches. The suggestion of how the so-called 'minster system' developed into the parish system as it is found in the twelfth century is stated in this way by Jones: "The 'minster hypothesis' sees a comprehensive network of minsters in control of other churches in their territories, to which slowly and reluctantly over the next several centuries they gave up parochial authority and sources of income. Parishes therefore evolved from the break-up and decay of minster territories."[31]

In the minster hypothesis the pattern of pastoral care provided through the minster churches began to change as lay landholders established private churches.[32] This development did not take place through the initiative of ecclesiastical authority, it simply reflected social changes that were taking place.[33] Pounds, along with others, sees the break up of the royal estate as being at the heart of this transition. The land became broken up into smaller units (ultimately manors) as local lords (*thegns*) acquired titles to the land later in the Anglo-Saxon period.[34] These *thegns* then took the initiative in founding churches on their estates. They were keen to do this because the tithe payments due to each

---

[31] Jones, *A Thousand Years of the English Parish*, p 40. Similar descriptions of this process may be found elsewhere: eg S. Bassett, 'Church and Diocese in the West Midlands: The Transition from British to Anglo-Saxon Control', in J. Blair and R. Sharpe (eds), *Pastoral Care before the Parish*, pp 13-40, pp 19-20.
[32] Pounds, *A History of the English Parish*, p 22.
[33] Pounds, *A History of the English Parish*, p 25; Spencer, *Parochial Vision*, p 5.
[34] Pounds, *A History of the English Parish*, pp 21, 25.

church began to be enforced by royal authority. Jones places this development in the middle of the tenth century.[35] There were therefore economic benefits in being in possession of a church,[36] and this is why Spencer goes so far as to say that the royal enforcement of the tithe ensured the development of the parochial system.[37] Pounds also sees the transition from earlier Anglo-Saxon patterns of scattered settlement towards predominately nucleated villages as an important factor in breaking up the earlier *parochiae* of the minster churches. However he notes that this change in settlement patterns may itself have been a consequence of the disintegration of the royal domain.[38] In sum, the minster hypothesis sees the parish system as developing in tandem with the social changes that produced the feudal system which was in place by the late eleventh century.

Yet we must be very careful of seeing uniformity where there was in fact great diversity. Pounds warns that the word 'system' is a misnomer and stresses that the reality was complex and varied.[39] Jones goes still further. She warns that the dominance of the parish in record keeping since the middle of the sixteenth century[40] obscures the more ancient patchwork of townships which lay behind the formation of parishes. She therefore argues that it is a mistake to identify parishes too closely with medieval manors. Jones stresses that townships were a territorial division of the resources of the

---

[35] Jones, *A Thousand Years of the English Parish*, pp 48-49. She states that by 930 the payment of tithes was obligatory and that this law was made effective by King Edgar soon after he became king in 959.
[36] Pounds, *A History of the English Parish*, p 29.
[37] Spencer, *Parochial Vision*, p 6.
[38] Pounds, *A History of the English Parish*, p 26.
[39] Pounds, *A History of the English Parish*, pp 21-22.
[40] Jones, *A Thousand Years of the English Parish*, p 22.

countryside, evident in the fact that place names survived even when there were no inhabitants in the land unit. The Latin word for township was *villa* which was then anglicised as 'vill'. This, however, was an administrative unit and by the tenth century it was assumed that every person belonged to a vill. The Domesday book was based on these vills and it was the vill that was the main administrative unit for centuries.[41] Jones warns us therefore that "parish boundaries reflected many stages in the development of English society."[42]

Jones acknowledges that while township and parish coincided in much of the south and in fertile areas of the north,[43] the patterns were very different elsewhere. It is this diversity which must make us cautious when speaking of the minster system or the minster hypothesis. Jones argues strongly that various different patterns and processes lie behind the development of parishes. This variety reflects the complex development of society in England.

Jones identifies the classic minster pattern as one in which the community sent out priests to serve chapels in the villages and hamlets in its area,[44] yet she illustrates this with the rather exceptional example of Worcester. This was an area where it is entirely possible that the Christianity community had survived among the British since Roman times. Bassett argues that St Helen's Worcester was the see of a British bishop, and that the incoming pagan Anglo-Saxons could have been converted to Christianity through this British

---

[41] Jones, *A Thousand Years of the English Parish*, p 22-23.
[42] Jones, *A Thousand Years of the English Parish*, p 24.
[43] Jones, *A Thousand Years of the English Parish*, p 23.
[44] Jones, *A Thousand Years of the English Parish*, p 42.

church.[45] The Norman cathedral later found it very difficult to establish authority over St Helen's and its attendant chapels.

Jones describes another pattern in which the minster appointed clergy to live locally and serve chapels. These chapels could have readily become independent as time proceeded such that there is no need to invoke the establishment of private chapels to account for the pattern of the later parish system. Jones calls this the Gallic pattern because this practice may have been brought to south-east England from Gaul. She illustrates this pattern through the names and history of the 'Nine Parishes' of South Elmham in Suffolk.[46]

In the Gilsland area of Cumbria Jones identifies what she terms an 'Irish' pattern of pastoral care in which there were numerous, independent, smaller churches. Gilsland was predominantly Celtic for centuries and did not become English until 1158. It had a monastery in Bewcastle but that community did not appear to have any authority over the other churches. This pattern of pastoral care is called 'Irish' because in Celtic Ireland the church appears to have been organised in a very different way. In the seventh and eighth centuries the Celtic church in Ireland was structured in relation to numerous small kingdoms, each of which had a bishop. There were possibly as many as 150 bishops at this

---

[45] Bassett, *Church and Diocese in the West Midlands*, pp 13-40, p 25.
[46] Jones, *A Thousand Years of the English Parish*, pp 45-46.

time[47] and there is evidence for a wide distribution of churches in this period.[48]

The point that stands out from this survey of the evidence during this period is simply the sheer variety in the organisation of pastoral care and mission that it expresses. It is not possible to account for the evidence by postulating tidy systems, even of minsters, before the twelfth century. One suspects that the desire to find such tidy systems is in itself the expression of a conviction that organisation rather than the calibre of spiritual leadership is more important in the delivery of effective pastoral care. The untidy surprises that Anglo-Saxon Christianity always springs upon us are particularly evident in the list of Irish bishops whom Jones notes were founding churches and operating in south-east England *alongside* the bishops of the mission stemming from Gregory I.[49] Such an overlap of mission activity is disturbing to those who expect clear geographical boundaries to be essential for effective Christian ministry. This period before the twelfth century is therefore well summed up by John Blair and Richard Sharpe:

"Much of this book emphasizes the secular context of pastoral organization: monasteria were founded by rulers, they often adjoined (and sometimes served as) centres of royal power, and their areas of responsibility were defined according to tribal, political or economic territories. One reason why the early insular church eludes the canon

---

[47] Jones, *A Thousand Years of the English Parish*, p 46. R. Sharpe, 'Churches and Communities in Early Medieval Ireland: Towards a Pastoral Model', in J. Blair and R. Sharpe (eds), *Pastoral Care before the Parish*, pp 81-109, p 107.
[48] Sharpe, *Churches and Communities in Early Medieval Ireland*, p 87.
[49] Jones, *A Thousand Years of the English Parish*, p 38.

lawyer's definitions is that it was articulated to the diverse forms of early insular lay society, and changed with them."[50]

Pastoral care and mission from the twelfth century onwards

Although the 'cold hand of canon law' froze the pattern of parishes from the twelfth century onwards[51] it must not be assumed that the financial circumstances that led to this state of affairs produced a uniform pattern of pastoral care all over England from this time on. Parochial boundaries were certainly fixed at this time because of the inherent territoriality associated with the payment of the tithe, but that does not mean that each of the parishes thus delineated operated in a similar way. As this section shows, parishes have varied considerably in the way they worked and in the area they covered. What a parish meant and what it did could vary considerably within England. The parish was indeed "an institution of great complexity".[52]

After the twelfth century parochial status was as carefully guarded as parish boundaries. Until 1843 it was impossible to create a new parish except by Act of Parliament.[53] Parochial status generally involved having a font and a graveyard.[54] This gives a clue as to why such status was so zealously protected. Once again it was money that was intimately linked with being a parish. The fees gained from such ministry would not be lightly given away to another

---

[50] Blair and Sharpe, *Introduction*, p 10.
[51] Jones, *A Thousand Years of the English Parish*, p 49.
[52] Jones, *A Thousand Years of the English Parish*, p 37.
[53] N. Scotland, *Evangelical Anglicans in a Revolutionary Age 1789-1901* (Paternoster, Carlisle: 2004) p 373.
[54] Pounds, *A History of the English Parish*, p 81.

18

church since that would threaten the very existence of the original church.

In order to modify the rigidities of the parochial system that these financial concerns engendered, many chapels were founded during the medieval period.[55] The word 'chapel' is nowadays associated with nonconformity following its appropriation for this purpose from the seventeenth century onwards, but in origin the word was Frankish and gained currency through William the Conquerors laws as being a term for a church that had no graveyard. In Anglo-Saxon times this would have been called a 'field church'.[56] However although some chapels do have their origins in adjustments to pre-Conquest patterns of pastoral care, the majority of chapels were indeed founded in the later-medieval period to relieve stresses created by the rigidities of the parish system.

Chapels created in the medieval period were often chapels of ease. These were generally established to provide for communities who lived some distance from the parish church or for areas in which the population had greatly expanded.[57] However there were also private chapels, oratories and chantries. Private chapels were not open to the public and could serve the residence of a wealthy family or an institution such as a gild or hospital. They were a means by which social differentiation and alternative human networks found spiritual expression. Although chantries were founded for the unbiblical purpose of saying masses for the dead they could also have other secondary functions. They might be the

[55] Jones, *A Thousand Years of the English Parish*, p 121.
[56] Jones, *A Thousand Years of the English Parish*, p 120.
[57] Pounds, *A History of the English Parish*, p 81.

focus of a gild and thus have a social role. A chantry endowment might be a way in which the services of a parish could be extended.[58] They might, for example, be a means of making more priests available to serve in a parish. Chantries were often simply associated with an altar or chapel within the parish church itself, but in a good number of cases they were actually independent church buildings. Because of this, a more accessible ministry might develop from them to the people in the surrounding area.

We might be inclined to think that chapels were nonetheless a relatively minor feature of parish life and the parish system during this period. This is not true, however. Spencer goes so far as to say that there may have been more non-parochial than parochial churches in medieval England.[59] This demonstrates that, while parish boundaries were fixed, the pattern of pastoral care in the past is very far from what is commonly assumed today. For example in Cornwall before the Reformation there were three times as many chapels as there were parish churches.[60] The explanation for this state of affairs lies in the conformity of Cornwall to the Irish or Celtic pattern of pastoral care and the late date at which English rule became effective in the area.

The north is the other region where chapels were particularly important. Northern parishes were notably larger than their southern counterparts. This is often because moorland and other barren areas were incorporated within their bounds. However the greater size of these northern parishes led to a very different system of operation in which

---

[58] Jones, *A Thousand Years of the English Parish*, p 128.
[59] Spencer, *Parochial Vision*, p 20.
[60] Jones, *A Thousand Years of the English Parish*, p 59.

chapels paid a large part. In Lancashire there were 100 chapels and 59 parishes in 1552.[61] Even as late as 1831 there were still northern parishes with large numbers of chapels.[62] Kendal had fifteen chapelries (that is, a district or area associated with a chapel), Prestbury twelve, Whalley eleven and Bakewell nine. In most of Cumbria there were large parishes associated with the name Kirby and it has been said that a full parochial system in the southern sense never really developed there until it was imposed by reorganisation in nineteenth and twentieth centuries.[63]

One might wonder whether the upheaval of the Reformation would have altered the parish system. The suppression of the chantries certainly gave an opportunity to redirect confiscated resources. However it seems that in the south many chapels simply disappeared, whereas in the north local inhabitants set about maintaining their much needed chapels themselves. An opportunity to alter the parochial structure was therefore missed as the church "stuck grimly to its obsolescent boundaries".[64] The growth of towns and the founding of new towns after the twelfth century also provided an occasion for addressing the rigidity of the parochial system. Again it was not taken. The creation of a new parish required great influence with church authorities, so in most cases new towns were only supplied by chapels of ease.[65] Of course some town-dwellers could also avail themselves of the non-parochial services offered by chapels and the other

[61] Jones, *A Thousand Years of the English Parish*, p 143.
[62] Jones, *A Thousand Years of the English Parish*, p 22.
[63] Jones, *A Thousand Years of the English Parish*, p 99, quoting from D.M. O'Sullivan's research regarding pre-conquest settlement patterns in Cumbria.
[64] Jones, *A Thousand Years of the English Parish*, p 136.
[65] Pounds, *A History of the English Parish*, pp 138-141.

institutions mentioned above. In the nineteenth century the problem of urban population growth reached crisis proportions for the parish system but the Church of England's response to this will be considered in Chapter 3.

One more feature of the parish system which tended to reinforce its rigidity and its all consuming importance is the way in which it accumulated what we today would call civil administrative functions. We have already seen that alternative units of social organisation such as the manor or vill (township) existed at an early date. However as the medieval period progressed it was the parish that became the focus of civil government. This can be illustrated through the development of the office of churchwarden. Wardens first appear as elected representatives of parishioners during the thirteenth century.[66] More and more tasks were placed upon their shoulders, to the extent that by the sixteenth and seventeenth centuries further parish officials such as the constable, overseer and surveyor had to be created and the wardens then tended to revert to their original responsibilities for the church.[67] This process demonstrates the way in which from the sixteenth century onwards the parish was the key unit of civil administration. From then until the nineteenth century the parish was all important, not just in the ecclesiastical domain but also in the social sphere. Indeed during the great period of reform in the 1830s it was the dominance of the parish in local government that left the Church of England dangerously exposed to the consequences

---

[66] Pounds, *A History of the English Parish*, p 184.
[67] Pounds, *A History of the English Parish*, pp 185, 193.

of social unrest.[68] However the reality today is that in most areas of England civil parishes no longer exist and where they do remain those administrative functions are completely divorced from church affairs. The secular forces which reinforced the parish system for so many centuries have now disappeared.

Conclusions

This brief survey of the provision of pastoral care and the practice of mission in past centuries leads us to note a number of aspects of the parish system.

(i) If the parish system is envisaged in terms of clearly defined geographical boundaries then the original reason for those boundaries has disappeared. The boundaries and parochial status of a church were of vital importance when the financial support of parish churches depended upon them, and we have seen that the unfortunate rigidity of the parochial system stemmed from this financial linkage. Nowadays however this link no longer exists and the necessity for such rigid boundaries and status is not there. The ancient system of tithes was dismantled in the nineteenth century and all remaining tithes were abolished in 1936. More recently, fees from weddings and funerals have become only a minor factor in the income and support of most churches. The Church of England as a whole does not rely upon fee income to support its pastoral care and

---

[68] Jones, *A Thousand Years of the English Parish*, pp 163-164. A. Burns, *The Diocesan Revival in the Church of England c.1800-1870* (Oxford University Press, Oxford: 1999) p 4.

outreach. It now relies largely upon the committed giving of current congregations.[69]

(ii) If the parish system is conceived in a more general way as a means of providing pastoral care and bringing the gospel to all then we must note how varied that provision has been in the past. The system as presently constituted is not the only way of practising Christian ministry. The most characteristic feature of the period before the twelfth century was that there was no clear system at all (though that does not mean that pastoral care and outreach was haphazard and disorganised). During that period such flexibility in organisation maintained a close link between the way society was organised and the way in which Christian mission was practised. From the twelfth century onwards we see that the rigidity of the parish system meant that chapels had to be founded in order to mitigate that rigidity. The danger signs for the church have been plain at various points since the twelfth century, but they were not heeded. A stress on organisation rather than sound teaching as being the key to Christian mission and ministry has created a gathering storm which is now battering the Church of England. It is this gathering storm which we examine in the next chapter.

---

[69] Thus the Church of England website
(http://www.cofe.anglican.org/info/funding/index.html, accessed 23 March 2005) reports that £600 million of the Church's annual income of £900 million comes through the parishes. Only £30 million comes from fees paid for weddings and funerals.

Chapter Three:

The Gathering Storm:

The Growing Inadequacies of the Parish System

Today when we look at the results of the 1851 Religious Census we are impressed by the overall numbers for church attendance as well as the particular figures for the Church of England.[70] It is a measure of how little we appreciate the immensity of the current mission task that we find it hard to comprehend the shock and gloom that this Census created at the time. It was perhaps confirming what many had suspected to be the real state of affairs, but it was a shock nonetheless. It revealed that there were vast numbers of people who were unreached and that nonconformity had grown enormously.[71] It is said that this Census has led to "an interpretative tradition concentrating on the scale of absenteeism" which only now is being reassessed and reversed to underline the achievements of Victorian religious energies.[72] However this reassessment cannot ignore the

---

[70] Jones, *A Thousand Years of the English Parish*, pp 267-268 gives some details and concludes that "at the most optimistic, half of those who could did go to church, and of that number only half went to the Church of England".

[71] For a particular county one can take Lincolnshire where in 1851 there were 705 Methodist chapels compared with 657 Anglican churches. Of those attending a place of worship on the census Sunday, 46% went to Methodist chapels and 43% to the established church. And this was the situation in a county which did not really see heavy industrialisation. See N.R. Wright, *Lincolnshire Towns and Industry 1700-1914* (History of Lincolnshire Committee for the Society for Lincolnshire History and Archaeology, Lincoln: 1982) p 238. Note also Spencer, *Parochial Vision*, p 36.

[72] Burns, *The Diocesan Revival in the Church of England*, p 5.

reality that at the time the figures were seen as clear evidence of failure of mission. Such a modern reinterpretation really only serves to underline the change in climate in the intervening 150 years.

The rigidity of the parish system is not the only reason for the failings revealed in 1851 but it was a significant factor. The inflexibility of the parish system and its financial basis led to both structural and theological strains upon the mission work of the Church of England. This chapter examines how both these elements contributed to the gathering storm which now threatens the entire institution with collapse.[73] Once again we observe a variety of attempts to do effective Christian mission within a conservative atmosphere which was deeply reluctant to change inherited systems of organisation.

It is commonly recognised that the pressures of population increase and industrialisation, along with the development of faster means of transport, placed significant strains on the parish system during the nineteenth century. However there is little recognition that theological diversity also played an increasing part in the growing ineffectiveness of the parish system. That is why both the structural (or social) and theological strains on the system need to be studied. Indeed they relate to one another. For example Nigel Scotland quotes Alan Gilbert as saying that the period from 1740-1830 was a disaster for the Church of England.[74] The implication appears to be that the structural strains on the system were then recognised and addressed in the period that followed.

---

[73] Edward Norman for example says "Not much force would be needed to flatten the Church of England as a coherent religious institution. It is a house of cards." Norman, *Anglican Difficulties,* p xiii.

[74] Scotland, *Evangelical Anglicans in a Revolutionary Age,* p 370.

However a number of people are now recognising that the response to the deficiencies at that time was the wrong one.[75] There was a focus on buildings and church accommodation rather than actual ministry which arguably arose from an erroneous theological perception about the nature of Christian mission and ministry which was gaining ground at the time.

In this chapter we will first consider the period before c. 1800 in order to show that both social and theological strains were already being felt within the parish system. We will then move on to the period after 1800 in which both industrialisation and theological turmoil made some sort of response to the system's inadequacies imperative. We will then look at the response that was made and assess its effectiveness.

Social and theological strains prior to 1800

The growth of towns after the fixing of the parochial system in the twelfth century provided the first strains upon it. We have already seen that provision was not easy to make (see above pp 21-22), especially in the case of towns that were entirely new.[76] There are hints even during the medieval period that social strains were not the only source of stress,

---

[75] Scotland, *Evangelical Anglicans in a Revolutionary Age*, pp 370-372. Jones, *A Thousand Years of the English Parish*, p 283 clearly identifies how the response can be seen as misdirected.

[76] See, for example the discussion on the ways in which a new town might be adjusted to the pre-existing parochial pattern in Pounds, *A History of the English Parish*, pp 138-144

but that theological differences could have provided a reason for the foundation of some chapels.[77]

However it is probably the Puritan lectureship system which demonstrates the first significant attempt to tackle inadequacies in the parochial system. Beginning in the reign of Elizabeth I, a significant movement within the Church of England developed which sought to improve the effectiveness of the ministry practised within the country's parishes. Although some sought organisational change, the greater priority was always the provision of effective preachers.[78] Amongst the Puritans there was a recognition that the parochial system was failing to provide good preaching for the population. It was to deal with this deficiency that lectureships were started. Their intention was to supplement the deficiencies of the parochial system, whether those deficiencies arose from the failure of the system to cope with increasing population in towns, or whether those deficiencies arose from the inadequate ministry of those clergy established within the parochial system. Lectureships were often set up and paid for by the local authority.[79] One of the earliest lectureships was that of St Antholin's in London, probably established in the reign of Edward VI.[80] The

---

[77] Money and rights were surely not all that was involved in disputes between monasteries and parishes. See Jones, *A Thousand Years of the English Parish*, pp 115-119 on this relationship.

[78] Irvonwy Morgan stresses that "The essential thing in understanding the Puritans was that they were preachers before they were anything else" I. Morgan, *The Godly Preachers of the Elizabethan Church* (Epworth Press, London: 1965)   p 11. See also Jim Packer's contention is that "Puritanism was, at its heart, a movement of spiritual revival". See J.I. Packer, *Among God's Giants: Aspects of Puritan Christianity* (Kingsway, Eastbourne: 1991) p 44.

[79] Pounds, *A History of the English Parish*, p 152.

[80] Morgan, *The Godly Preachers of the Elizabethan Church*, p 49.

numbers that ultimately operated within a city like London show that they became a most significant pastoral provision.[81] The collapse of the lectureship system a hundred years later was largely because of the exclusion of those most likely to be employed in them after the Restoration of 1660. However they may also have been difficult to maintain simply because of the more insecure nature of their endowment.

It is notable that there were projects to reform the parish system to make it more pastorally effective occurred when Puritans gained political power during the Commonwealth. However we must note that the focus was not on parochial organisation as such but rather on the provision of learned and preaching ministers.[82] The plans to redistribute tithe income in order to achieve this end generated an opportunity to redraw parish boundaries. A survey was made for this purpose in 1649 and it is notable that it was organised by county rather than by diocese.[83] In northern counties recommendations were made to break up large parishes through making subordinate chapels parishes in their own right. However these plans to augment poor livings and

---

[81] P.S. Seaver, *The Puritan Lectureships: The Politics of Religious Dissent, 1560-1662* (Stanford University Press, Stanford CA: 1970) pp 121-170 has an excellent chapter describing the London lectureships and demonstrates clearly that they constituted a formidable institution. Seaver shows that by 1600 just about half of London's parishes hired lecturers: "In a city little more than a square mile in area and with a population of just under a quarter of a million, approximately one hundred sermons were preached each week by lecturers" (p 125). The peak was reached in the late 1620s when 116 London parishes (90% of the total) had records of hiring lecturers.

[82] Jones, *A Thousand Years of the English Parish*, p 173.

[83] Jones, *A Thousand Years of the English Parish*, p 174. In other words it was making social realities rather than historic tradition the determining factor for organising the church's mission.

reorganise medieval parish structures were abandoned after the Restoration in 1660.

This was of course a significant moment in the story of the parochial system. The failure to accommodate Puritan clergy and Puritan plans for reform following the 1662 Act of Uniformity meant that new forms of pastoral provision emerged through nonconformity. Indeed this sowed the seeds for the further undermining of the basis of the parochial system. The tithe had first been questioned in print in 1618,[84] but it was after 1650 that Quakers and others began to object to paying the tithe which was going to support a ministry that they did not want.[85]

If the parochial system itself could not be easily reformed under the pressure of social and theological strains, then the financial arrangements that underlay it could at least be modified to alleviate some of its effects. This was the purpose behind the establishment of Queen Anne's Bounty. In 1704 Parliament recognised the need for a scheme to help poorer clergy, possibly in part due to nonconformists' principled opposition to tithe.[86] Surveys were made to establish which livings were poor and the first augmentations were made under the scheme in 1714.[87]

A further significant development in the eighteenth century was the rise of Methodism. Today many find it strange that John Wesley and others met such bitter opposition to preaching in the parishes of others. In fact Wesley was encouraged to minister in this way through the influence of

---

[84] Pounds, *A History of the English Parish*, p 47.
[85] Jones, *A Thousand Years of the English Parish*, pp 179-180.
[86] Jones, *A Thousand Years of the English Parish*, p 155.
[87] Jones, *A Thousand Years of the English Parish*, p 156.

George Whitefield. They were moved to do so by the evident pastoral inadequacies that they encountered. It is the financial basis of the parochial system which provides an explanation for some of the hostility that they met. The rules they broke had been designed to protect that system and its financial underpinnings. It was not for nothing that Wesley is associated with the idea that the world was his parish. Although Wesley loved the Church of England and was initially tenacious about every point of decency and order, his heart for the gospel led him to that broader work.[88]

Social and theological strains from 1800 onwards

It is widely acknowledged that the massive growth in urban population produced intolerable social strains upon the parish system after 1800. In the early 1820s Birmingham, Sheffield and Manchester were single parishes with populations of the order of 120,000 in each.[89] There were 100,000 in the ancient Lancashire parish of Whalley.[90]

However the rigidities of the parish system had already led evangelicals to start taking initiatives in bringing the gospel to the nation. The movement to establish proprietary chapels in order to address the inadequacies of the parochial system

---

[88] A. Brown-Lawson, *John Wesley and the Anglican Evangelicals of the Eighteenth Century: : A Study in Cooperation and Separation With Special Reference to the Calvinistic Controversies* (Pentland, Edinburgh: 1994) pp 25-48 describes how Whitefield and the Wesleys came to adopt these methods. Brown-Lawson also notes that the term 'world parish' should be ascribed to Whitefield rather than John Wesley (p 39).
[89] Scotland, *Evangelical Anglicans in a Revolutionary Age*, p 337.
[90] Jones, *A Thousand Years of the English Parish*, p 187.

began in the late eighteenth century.[91] This movement is sometimes represented as primarily an attempt to create more pastoral provision for the growing numbers of people in towns and cities.[92] However the reality is far more complex. Certainly the glaring deficiency in pastoral provision provided opportunities for private initiative to be taken. It must be stressed that – like the private, proprietary churches that were being founded at the end of the Anglo-Saxon period (see above p 13) – these proprietary chapels were funded at private expense. They were not dependent in any way upon tithes or other historic endowments, most of their annual funding coming from pew rents. Although some seek to dismiss those who founded these chapels as motivated purely by financial gain, suggesting that the appointment of a popular preacher could provide a handsome income to the proprietor, the evidence is rather that other motives predominated. Usually the desire was simply to increase evangelical preaching ministry, as with the earlier Puritan lectureships.[93] They did indeed provide the basis for well known ministries such as Richard Cecil and Daniel Wilson at St John's Bedford Row,[94] but the fact that effective preaching produced generous giving does not mean that these chapels were founded primarily for financial gain. Sometimes they were created to reach the

---

[91] For an account of the origins of many proprietary chapels see B.F.L. Clarke, *The Building of the Eighteenth-Century Church* (SPCK, London: 1963) pp 187-199.
[92] J.H. Overton, *The English Church in the Nineteenth Century (1800-1833)* (Longmans, London: 1894) p 144.
[93] E. Stock, *The History of the Church Missionary Society Vol I* (Church Missionary Society, London: 1899) pp 43-44 gives a survey of the main preachers around the year 1800.
[94] G.R. Balleine, *A History of the Evangelical Party in the Church of England* (Church Book Room Press, London: 1951) p 156.

upper classes who frequented particular districts or towns,[95] but again the wealth of those classes does not exclude the motivation of providing an evangelical ministry as being uppermost. It is true that these were strongholds of the evangelicals, but they were not exclusively so.

Once more, we see that it was theological strains (in this case the hostility that many evangelicals met in exercising their ministry) as well as social ones which led to this initiative designed to circumvent the rigidities of the parochial system. By 1824 there may have been as many as 59 proprietary chapels in London and 200 in the country as a whole.[96] As time went by these chapels were often incorporated into the parochial system as part of the general response to the strains placed upon that system, and evangelicals did recognise that they had their disadvantages.[97] Furthermore as the nineteenth century progressed the work of these chapels appears to have become even more motivated by theological controversy. Many developed into providing ministry for those who found the theological innovations of Tractarianism intolerable.[98]

Proprietary chapels were one initiative which arose because of the social and theological strains affecting the parochial system. However the degree of strain meant that

---

[95] S.E.A. Green, *St James' Ryde* (Ffrancon Press, Ryde: 1975) gives the account of one such initiative.
[96] Scotland, *Evangelical Anglicans in a Revolutionary Age*, p 375.
[97] Scotland, *Evangelical Anglicans in a Revolutionary Age*, p 376. Overton, *The English Church in the Nineteenth Century*, p 147.
[98] See for example M. Longham, *Buxton: A People's History* (Pentland Press, Lancaster: 2001) pp 149-159 on Trinity Chapel in Buxton, and J. Dearing, *The Church That Would Not Die* (Baron Birch, Whittlebury: 1993) on St Mary's Castle Street in Reading.

the challenge needed to be addressed in a far more comprehensive manner. After the decisive defeat of Napoleon at Waterloo the country was able to place its focus on internal issues such as this. We must note that the response to the strains in the parochial system essentially focussed on building more churches and creating new parishes, even though attention was also paid to the increase in stipends, the erection of vicarages and the provision of theological training.[99] When Parliament's attention was drawn to the inadequacy of churches in populous areas it granted money and passed Acts to enable churches to be built through the Church Building Commissioners. The gravity of the problem was illustrated by the situation in London. In the London area outside the City there was a population of 1,129,451 in 1818, yet the churches and episcopal chapels could only accommodate 151,536. The net result of this effort was that across England during the period 1818-1856 the Church Building Commissioners built 615 churches.[100]

A further impetus to relieving the strains in the parish system was produced when Robert Peel became Prime Minister in 1841. Social unrest, seen for example in the Chartists, was thought to be a consequence of the failings of the Church of England in manufacturing districts.[101] In response, an Act was passed 1843 which made it easier to create new parishes. Previously the subdivision of large

---

[99] Jones, *A Thousand Years of the English Parish*, pp 217-237.
[100] Jones, *A Thousand Years of the English Parish*, p 263. Spencer, *Parochial Vision*, p 34 gives overall figures of 612 new parishes and nearly 2000 new churches being built during this approximate period. Of course, not all new church buildings were as a result of the efforts of the Church Building Commissioners.
[101] Jones, *A Thousand Years of the English Parish*, p 264.

industrial parishes had been a slow process,[102] but this legislative change greatly accelerated the process of creating new parishes and districts. In the first two years after the Act 194 new parishes and districts were prepared.[103]

However this predominant strategy of erecting more church buildings and establishing more parishes was not the only possible response. Jones calls her chapter describing this response to the strains in the parish system *The Triumph of the Parish*. By this she is ironically indicating how under these pressures there was no attempt to rethink the parochial system for urban areas. The basic parochial structure was accepted, perhaps because the vested financial interests were so strong. However this meant that just at the point when the basic parochial structure was being superseded in civil affairs, the church was not willing to think more radically about its mission.[104] From the beginning, the response to the strains in the parish system was obsessed with the issue of church accommodation, i.e. with the number of seats provided through church buildings. Geoffrey Best highlights the influence that Richard Yates had on the issue of church reform between 1780 and 1830.[105] It was Yates who was largely responsible for bringing the shortage of church accommodation to the attention of the public and Parliament.[106] Significantly, though, there was little attention

---

[102] Scotland, *Evangelical Anglicans in a Revolutionary Age*, p 373. The struggle to create new parochial structures prior to this Act in various large cities is described in Jones, *A Thousand Years of the English Parish*, pp 267-283.
[103] Jones, *A Thousand Years of the English Parish*, p 267.
[104] Jones, *A Thousand Years of the English Parish*, p 264.
[105] G.F.A. Best, *Temporal Pillars: Queen Anne's Bounty, the Ecclesiastical Commissioners, and the Church of England* (Cambridge University Press, Cambridge: 1964) p 147.
[106] Best, *Temporal Pillars*, p 148.

paid to the more fundamental question of how one reached the people who were supposed to fill the seats as this new church accommodation was being provided. Scotland points out that while evangelicals were good parish men, most failed to recognise the failings and confines of the parish system.[107] Later on evangelicals did begin to see the difficulties. Thus Ryle's remarks in 1882 about the danger of making an idol out of the parish system (see above p 1) were made in the course of an address which sought to outline a strategy for getting people into the many new church buildings.[108] Even the high churchman Walter F. Hook reflected later on whether the scheme of subdividing the great parish of Leeds (where he was vicar) which he had pursued with such enthusiasm had really been for the best.[109] One need not sympathise with his desire to go back to the old system and make the vicar of Leeds a bishop with 20-30 clergy, in order to appreciate what he had realised. However such doubts were largely ignored.

It needs to be appreciated that the inadequate response to the strains placed on the parochial system during the nineteenth century had at base a theological and ecclesiological rationale. It was not mere pragmatism. The failure to question the parish system itself within the large

---

[107] Scotland, *Evangelical Anglicans in a Revolutionary Age*, p 370-371. Scotland cites Sumner and Shaftesbury as exceptions however.
[108] Ryle, *Can They be Brought in?*, p 28. Scotland notes Bishop Anthony Thorold making a similar point in 1874 (Scotland, *Evangelical Anglicans in a Revolutionary Age*, p 371).
[109] Jones, *A Thousand Years of the English Parish*, pp 272-274. Jones also records how Gilbert Scott the younger spoke of the division of parishes in Leeds having been carried a great deal too far (Jones, *A Thousand Years of the English Parish*, p 283), even though the reason for this comment was Scott's preference for large church buildings.

towns and cities was partly because that system was beginning to be seen as an important element in Anglican identity (a subject discussed in the next chapter). Arthur Burns queries the traditional understanding that the Tractarians were responsible for the renewal of diocesan life and the ministry of the bishop. However in placing what he calls the Diocesan Revival as occurring from the 1820s onwards he still argues that it was the orthodox high-churchmen who predominated in this movement he wishes to record. He sees this Diocesan Revival as existing in parallel to the efforts outlined above of the Ecclesiastical Commission. The common elements of concern in this diocesan reform movement are significant. Burns says that the chief concerns were "A concentration on local administrative structures; the development of unity and community spirit both as an important objective in its own right and as a means to others; and a respect for the existing and historic institutions of the Church as the building-blocks of a response to new challenges".[110] It can be seen therefore that the response to the strains in the parish system at both diocesan and national level saw organisational and structural solutions as being the way forward. Whether the impetus came from orthodox high-churchmen or Tractarians, there was a failure to see that retaining the basic parochial structure was not the only way forward. At just the time when the parish system was being discarded in the civil government of towns, there was no similar vision in the Church of England for seeing its organisation as existing to serve the greater priority of Christian mission to the people of England.

---

[110] Burns, *The Diocesan Revival in the Church of England*, p 262.

Meanwhile, concurrent with the response which saw adjusting and improving the parish system as the way to cope with the strains upon it, the theological strains within the Church of England were increasing. After the arrival of the Tractarians, the party spirit increased. This meant that evangelicals were frequently suspicious of proposed changes in organisation simply because of from where the proposed reforms originated. Burns describes how such party spirit hindered the Diocesan Revival.[111]

There was one other social factor that could have placed increasing strains on the parish system at this time. It is surprising how accounts of the social changes of the nineteenth century in relation to the parish system tend to focus simply on the increase of population. Nevertheless another great social change from the 1840s onwards was the coming of the railways and other improved means of transport. The greater mobility that this allowed surely enabled the growing theological diversity to be expressed at least in the churchgoing habits of the middle classes. Even though parish boundaries continued to be as rigid as ever, theological differences (and indeed an increase in sceptical liberalism) meant that people were more and more willing to cross those boundaries in order to attend a church which was more in sympathy with their own views. Thus Ryle in 1882 expresses every sympathy with families who choose to attend church in another parish because of the unsound doctrine taught in their own local church.[112]

---

[111] Burns, *The Diocesan Revival in the Church of England*, p 265.
[112] Ryle, *Can They be Brought in?*, pp 21-22.

Conclusion

By focussing on those adjustments to the parish system which augmented the number of buildings and parishes it is easy to assume that the Church of England successfully adapted to the social and theological strains that were placed upon the inherited parochial structure during the nineteenth century. Indeed many today think that this is the case. However this understanding must be questioned, particularly in the light of the Victorians' own interpretation of the failures revealed by the 1851 census. They were bothered by figures which showed that there were more Methodist buildings than Church of England in areas such as Lincolnshire. The weakened influence of the Church of England in counties like Cornwall did concern them. Many bishops were alarmed by the lack of impact in the cities. Certainly a variety of new mission initiatives did take place in this period but none succeeded in radically reforming the parish system and changing this overall picture.

The reason why the nineteenth century response to the rigidities of the parish system can be seen as successful today is probably because within the nineteenth century another development was taking place that redefined the Church of England. As the century went on the claims of the Church of England to be the church of the nation grew weaker and weaker. Between 1800 and 1900 the Church of England was transformed from being a national church into a leading denomination. As a large denomination the Church of England could be seen as successful and the parish system as being relatively effective. As a national church with an effective outreach and pastoral care for the people of England, however, it was a failure. Merely adapting the rigidities of the parish system to social and theological strains was not sufficient if it aspired to be such a national church. It is significant that it was during the nineteenth century that the term 'Anglicanism' gained currency. That term is a denominational label. In the next chapter we must examine how structural features of the Church of England such as the parochial system have come to be cherished and one might even say idolised within Anglicanism today.

Chapter Four:

The Parish System and Anglicani sm

Edward Norman well expresses the commonly held view about the Church of England and the role of parishes today: "Parochial ministry has been thought to be Anglicanism *par excellence*; the heart of the whole enterprise".[113] If this is intended to underline the fundamental importance of local church ministry then such a view is to be commended. However those words are more likely to be read as reflecting the way in which Anglican identity nowadays is bound up with what is called the parish system. Thus in considering the name 'Church of England' the Bishop of Bradwell, Laurie Green, claims that it speaks of the importance of being incarnational. And he declares that it is "that incarnational genius which determines that we should be a parochially structured Church".[114] In similar vein Simon Parke sees the parish system as at the heart of what can give hope to the future of the Church of England. He describes it as "the physical expression of God in community".[115] Interestingly Martin Cavender (Director of the *Springboard* initiative) can see that the parish system has been adulterated into the defence of territorial boundaries, but can still state that "the Proprietary Chapel is a Victorian hangover and is simply intended to set outside true Anglican ecclesiology a

---

[113] Norman, *Anglican Difficulties*, p 142.
[114] L. Green, *President's address by the Bishop of Bradwell to Chelmsford Diocesan Synod: 8 November 2003*.
[115] S.Parke, *Commentary on Church Times Survey 22 Feb 2002* (http://www.churchtimes.co.uk/churchtimes/website/pages.nsf/httppublicpages/7A23EA7E78BD9B2580256FA200114350, accessed 23 March 2005).

patriarchal arrangement for trust provision for a given area".[116] It is this identification of the parish system with Anglicanism that will be examined in this chapter. Inevitably this means looking at the development of the concept of Anglicanism, the question of Anglican identity, and the sense in which the parish system can be linked to that identity.

The development of Anglicanism

It surprises many to realise that 'Anglicanism' is a term that appears to have been invented during the 1830s.[117] Of course that does not mean that there was no Church of England before that date, it is rather an indicator that this term was expressing a changing understanding of what the Church of England was and should be.

At the time of the Reformation the Church of England was understood to be the continued manifestation of Christianity within the nation of England, a manifestation which had needed reforming to rid itself of earlier abuses and unbiblical teachings and practice. Any other expression of Christianity within England was, however, inconceivable, as was any concept of an international Anglicanism in which Church of England practice was emulated in other nations.[118]

---

[116] M. Cavender, *A New Legal Framework, Part 1*, National Anglican Church Planting Conference, 20 June 2002
(http://www.encountersontheedge.org.uk/main/Reports/HTB/framework1.htm, accessed 23 March 2005).
[117] P.Avis, 'What is Anglicanism?', in S. Sykes, J. Booty, and J. Knight (eds) *The Study of Anglicanism* (SPCK, London: 1998) pp 459-476, pp 460-461. Norman, *Anglican Difficulties*, p xii.
[118] M. Burkill, *Lambeth 1998 - The Death of Anglicanism?*, Churchman 113 (1999) pp 30-47, p 32; J.P. Richardson, *'To Our Own People Only': Re-owning Original Anglicanism*, Churchman 112 (1998) pp 124-130, p 127. Note also how this understanding is expressed in the Preface to the Book of Common Prayer.

This is why John Richardson, for example, underlines the point of Bishop Stephen Neill that 'Anglican' was originally a geographical rather than a theological term.[119] This does not mean that there is no 'Anglican theology' but rather there are no special 'Anglican doctrines'. In other words the Church of England was in the business of mere Christianity and did not want to make the mistake of enforcing assent to secondary features of Christian teaching. While many of the 39 Articles insist on subscription to key Christian doctrines, Article XXXIV famously states "It is not necessary that Traditions and Ceremonies be in all places one, and utterly alike". This self-understanding is very far removed from today's distaste for doctrinal precision and discipline which is then combined with a stress on secondary features of Christian practice.

It can be argued that the Reformation understanding of the Church of England began to be altered as time went on because of debates surrounding the role of bishops. It is possible that the insistence in some quarters on the necessity of bishops ultimately led to the idea of Anglicanism. Thus the imposition of Episcopacy in 1662 and the Great Ejection of nearly 2000 ministers was responsible for the growth of a body of Christians (apart from Roman Catholics) whose relationship with the structures of the Church of England became looser and looser as time went by. It is notable that the Anglicans in Scotland today are found in the Scottish *Episcopal* Church. It had proved impossible to force bishops on Scotland so in that country it was a body which insisted on bishops that formed the dissent from the majority Christian community.

---

[119] Richardson, *'To Our Own People Only'*, p 125.

However another significant step towards creating what we see as Anglicanism today was taken following the achievement of independence by the American colonies. In these colonies the variety of church order that had been excluded in England itself in 1662 was tolerated, including places like Virginia where the colony was ordered in accordance with the practice of the Church of England. While the American colonies were governed from England, there were no bishops physically present. Even amongst those whom we might term Anglicans there was opposition to consecrating a bishop because the role of a bishop was so bound up with English political control. However when that political control was broken by the American Revolution a means of exercising ultimate control of the 'Anglican' churches had to be found. It was by no means assumed that this should be through bishops, but in the end some Connecticut clergy elected Samuel Seabury to be their bishop and had him consecrated in Scotland in 1784.[120] It is significant that the insistence on bishops was then expressed in the way these Christians congregations became known as the Protestant *Episcopal* Church in the USA.

In the early nineteenth century the development of the British Empire and further colonies overseas again raised the question of the status of those who adhered to the order of the Church of England beyond English shores. By 1841 there were ten diocesan sees established outside Britain and

---

[120] See for example the accounts in W.L. Sachs *The Transformation of Anglicanism: From State Church to Global Communion* (Cambridge University Press, Cambridge: 1993) p 67, and W.M. Jacob *The Making of the Anglican Church Worldwide* (SPCK, London: 1997) pp 62-72.

the USA.[121] In many places the Anglicans who settled abroad were living alongside Presbyterians, Methodists and other nonconformists. These circumstances naturally led to a search for Anglican identity. The rise of the Tractarian movement can be seen as seeking to stress a distinctive Anglican identity and its influence is seen by 1840 in the appeal to establish a Colonial Bishoprics Fund. The appeal was underpinned by the desire to see the "full benefits" of the Church of England's apostolical government and discipline being brought to the colonies.[122]

Thus developments overseas gave occasion for the particular order of the Church of England to be emphasised. These overseas developments were reinforced in the early nineteenth century by the strains on the national Church's life that we have discussed in Chapter 3. It was becoming increasingly evident with the growth of nonconformity and the failure to reach out with the gospel to the great urban populations that the claim of the Church of England to be the national Church was rather hollow. These factors combined to transform the Church of England into a denomination as the nineteenth century continued. Further denominational expressions can be seen in the establishment of synods and the Lambeth Conferences during the last half of that century. We can therefore understand why it was that the word 'Anglicanism' appeared during the 1830s. It is a term that is partly related to the response that the Church of England made to the failures of the parish system to deliver effective mission and pastoral care. It is a term which regrettably

---

[121] A record of some of these developments is to be found in Jacob *The Making of the Anglican Church Worldwide,* pp 85-104.
[122] Sachs *The Transformation of Anglicanism,* p 114, and Jacob *The Making of the Anglican Church Worldwide,* p 112.

stresses the secondary features of Christianity, matters which in the end are things indifferent. It is not a term that sits comfortably with the original ideals of the Church of England at the time of the Reformation which sought to comprehend all those who agreed on the fundamentals of the Christian faith and refused to insist on binding human consciences with such secondary matters.[123]

Anglican identity

It is therefore not surprising to find that it is only in the last 150 years or so that there has been such heart searching within the Church of England over the question of Anglican identity. The initial enterprise of establishing that Anglican identity focussed on reinterpreting the late-sixteenth-century Church of England as the *via media* with its chief architect as Richard Hooker. Many still cling to this identity despite historical studies which have shown the difficulties with this reading of Hooker.[124]

During the twentieth century the Anglican identity tended to be sought in a distinctive theological method. Thus Paul Avis states "On this interpretation, the distinctive identity of Anglicanism is located in the sphere of theological method and the understanding of authority that informs it,

---

[123] Richardson, *'To Our Own People Only'*, pp 129-130: "Anglicanism should be defined as 'a form of church order and practice derived by applying universal scriptural principles within a particular cultural context with the aim of effecting God's honour and people's godliness'. This may not be the answer people expect, recognize or accept, but it is the answer which produced the Church of England".
[124] N. Atkinson *Richard Hooker and The Authority of Scripture, Tradition and Reason: Reformed Theologian of the Church of England?* (Paternoster, Carlisle 1997).

rather than in terms of liturgy, spirituality or polity."[125] Stephen Sykes appears to think in similar terms when he says "But in almost all forms and expressions of the Anglican way, a certain character or spirit is evident which is the result of interconnecting Scripture, common worship and doctrine, and tending to make the whole serve the unity of the church."[126] Of course the use of the Book of Common Prayer also used to be seen as the source of Anglican identity, but in the last decades of the twentieth century this could no longer carry any conviction given the widespread use of other liturgies.[127]

However the case for locating Anglican identity in a theological method has been undermined in recent years by the battles within the Anglican Communion over first the ordination of women and then homosexuality. Perhaps in response to these issues, which in reality reflect deep theological divisions, there have been alternative attempts to locate Anglican identity simply in terms of inclusivity.[128] Such a contradictory inclusivity cannot stand for long unless the structures of Anglicanism are deployed to hold the

---

[125] Avis, *What is Anglicanism?*, p 475.
[126] S. Sykes, 'The Anglican Character', in I. Bunting (ed.) *Celebrating the Anglican Way* (Hodder & Stoughton, London: 1996) pp 21-32, p 32.
[127] Norman, *Anglican Difficulties,* pp 16-19. These theories which see unity through a common theological method or the Book of Common Prayer are noted in A. Redfern, *Being Anglican* (Darton Longman & Todd, London: 2000) p 9.
[128] Redfern, *Being Anglican,* p 9: "Anglicanism is about fundamentalisms in dialogue". T. Jenkins, 'Anglicanism: The only answer to Modernity', in D. Dormor, J. McDonald, and J. Caddick (eds) *Anglicanism: The Answer to Modernity* (Continuum, London: 2003) pp 186-205, p 191, states: "Anglicanism contains representative parties favouring order, freedom, and human well being. But the [Anglican] settlement insists that their holding together in a common human project is more important than their independent and sometimes incompatible claims to truth".

organisation together. In England at least we should not be surprised then to see that Anglican identity is becoming located in obedience to bishops, alongside a commitment to the financial structures and the parochial system. This is deeply ironic since it precisely inverts both the biblical place for these matters and the ideals of the Church of England settlement at the Reformation (see pp 45-46 above). To insist on the necessity of obedience in secondary matters of order and structure while abandoning all theological limits in the name of inclusivity and comprehensiveness is bizarre. At its most extreme this could lead to an insistence on obedience to parish boundaries while abandoning basic Christian theological boundaries altogether. This is why the parish system must not be tied to Anglican or Christian identity.

The parish system and Anglican identity

Everyone tends to think they know what they mean by the parish system but the reality concealed beneath the rhetorical use of this phrase can vary widely. For some the parish system will mean maintaining the historic territorial boundaries of parish churches. However we have already seen that those territories were in origin defined as part of a financial arrangement (for the support of parochial ministry) which no longer exists today in England.[129] Furthermore making the parish system in this sense an important component of Anglican identity is impossible because abroad

---

[129] "The parish boundaries often have meaning only when deciding who can or cannot be baptized or married in the church" G. Ecclestone (ed.) *The Parish Church?: Explorations in The Relationship of The Church and The World* (Mowbray, London: 1988) p 5.

such a definition is meaningless.[130] Many Anglican churches abroad do not operate in such terms at all.

More commonly the parish system is invoked to express an ideal of pastoral care and outreach to all. Hence the quotations above (p 41) which refer to the incarnational principle. It has been expressed as "an idea in the mind" rather than what actually happens.[131] But even this ideal of pastoral care expressed through the parish system can mean different things to different people. For some it means simply the principle of inclusivity at all costs.[132] Others however will see the parish system as giving "a sense of responsibility for mission and ministry to the whole community of the parish."[133]

There have been attempts to contrast alternative models of local churches as being associational or parish. In a book from the Grubb Institute the parish church is seen as being accountable to the local community and the parish boundary is seen as an aid in defining the extent of that accountability.[134] By contrast, in the 'associational' type of church the local community is seen primarily as offering potential for church growth. There is a recognition here that the traditional concept of the parish church must be adjusted. However the distinction intended by these two models does

---

[130] Redfern *Being Anglican*, pp 4-5. D. Sceats 'Orders and Officers of the Church', in I. Bunting (ed.) *Celebrating the Anglican Way*, pp 179-198 p 184. Furthermore Malcolm Brown in Toyne, *A Measure for Measures*, p 122 states: "In other parts of the Anglican Communion the parochial system is not even part of immediate inheritance".
[131] Ecclestone, *The Parish Church?*, p 5.
[132] Thus Redfern *Being Anglican*, p 4 declares: "Being Anglican involves a commitment to welcome and include all who live in each parish".
[133] Sceats, *Orders and Officers of the Church*, p 184.
[134] Ecclestone, *The Parish Church?*, pp 4-11.

not really work. There is nothing to stop those churches which make a clear distinction between the church and the world (in terms of membership) being open to the surrounding community, feeling a sense of responsibility for its welfare and being effective in engaging with it. Indeed that the reality of church life is far more complex is admitted within this same book.[135] It is of course recognised that there are so called associational churches in the sense defined there both inside and outside the Church of England. However the reverse holds true as well. One does not have to be Anglican in order to be a parish church in the sense that *The Parish Church?* defines it. Thus the parish system in this adjusted sense, while reflecting admirable ideals, cannot be linked to the definition of Anglican identity.

We are therefore left with the conclusion that the parish system is only bound up with Anglican identity by virtue of it being the current structure and organisation for ministering outreach and pastoral care through Anglican churches. Perhaps it is in this sense that Cavender finds proprietary chapels so anomalous in terms of Anglican ecclesiology.[136] However this position betrays a fear of modifying the existing parish system (even if boundaries are not seen as significant) which can only be disastrous for mission and ministry. It is even more inflexible than the parish system that emerged in the twelfth century. To marry this understanding of the parish system with Anglican identity would be catastrophic and ensure the eventual extinction of the Church of England.

---

[135] Ecclestone, *The Parish Church?* p 15.
[136] Cavender, *A New Legal Framework.*

Conclusion

This brief examination of the link between Anglicanism and the parish system demonstrates the need for a radical rethink. The modern concept of Anglicanism needs to be challenged. Trying to retain Anglican distinctives in the sense that has emerged over the past 150 years means that secondary matters of Christianity are emphasised to the detriment of the mission and ministry of the Church. This is especially so when the parish system (in whatever form it is understood) is incorporated into the definition of Anglican identity.

Essential Anglican identity needs to be sought in the determination to insist on the fundamentals of the Christian faith while refusing to make adherence to secondary matters compulsory. Of course this begs a lot of questions as to what is secondary and how such compulsion operates, but that must not make us neglect the vision. According to Richardson it is the vision of Anglicanism which Bishop Stephen Neill espoused.[137] It is an ecumenical vision which seeks to involve all Christian communities that adhere to Christian basics in reaching out to the people of England. Within that vision the parish system (or whatever term one wishes to give to the organisation of pastoral care and outreach) must be seen in its proper place. It is a servant of the church's mission. Inevitably structures and organisation are needed for effective mission, but making a particular form of structure essential to that mission is a big mistake. The identity of the Christian community must be located in the gospel and not in its form of church order, no matter how necessary such order is.

---

[137] Richardson, 'To Our Own People Only', pp 124-125.

Chapter Five:

The Parish System and Mission Today

Edward Norman sees the original territorial ideal expressed in the parish system and the notion of a National Church as being a noble one. Nevertheless he paints a scathing picture of the reality that exists today. He says that there is an inherent institutional conservatism which doggedly adheres to the parochial structure. He bemoans the fact that Church of England leaders have no other strategy to secure a religious presence than the style and form they have known all their lives. He speaks of the way in which changes in the nature of society have made the antiquated parochial units unable to identify suitable constituents to address.[138] Naturally these are generalisations, but it is a portrayal which reflects the issues and problems with the parish system that have been identified in this study. The storm has now hit the Church of England. The theological and social strains which appeared in the parish system in the early nineteenth century can no longer be hidden. The response which transformed the Church of England into the Anglican denomination and sought to cope by building more churches and subdividing parishes is now bankrupt. The statistics of pastoral care and outreach show that Anglicanism and the parish system as currently constituted simply do not deliver what they claim.

It is encouraging, then, to see that there are those within the Church of England who have recognised that this is indeed the case and are working towards addressing these

---

[138] Norman, *Anglican Difficulties,* pp 143-145.

immense issues. Spencer's book *Parochial Vision* identifies the deficiencies of the current system and suggests a response in the 'minster model'. The reports *Mission-Shaped Church* and *A Measure for Measures* show a similar concern, and there is a cautious recognition of the problem by the Archbishop of Canterbury.[139] Nevertheless it is this author's contention that these do not go far enough. The reason why the crisis is so bad is that the full extent of the theological and social problems besetting the parish system have not been appreciated. For Church of England congregations to be effective in mission and ministry today, both of those problems must be properly addressed.

The reality of theological diversity

The assumption that all Church of England churches are exercising a recognisably biblical and Christian ministry is widespread, but unfortunately it is not true. Comprehensiveness in the sense discussed above (p 43) is a properly biblical and Anglican ideal, but it cannot be redefined to cover those who deny fundamentals of the faith. An all-embracing inclusivism will not work[140] and is not consistent with the claim to be a Christian Church. The significance and impact of the theological diversity that Ryle observed over a century ago is now far worse. Acknowledging

---

[139] See the Archbishop of Canterbury's Presidential Address to General Synod on July 14 2003 (www.anglicancommunion.org/acns/articles/35/00/acns3507.html, accessed 23 March 2005): "In all kinds of places, the parochial system is working remarkably. It's just that we are increasingly aware of the contexts where it simply isn't capable of making an impact, where something has to grow out of it or alongside it, not as a rival... but as an attempt to answer questions that the parish system was never meant to answer".

[140] Spencer, *Parochial Vision*, p 109 appears to recognise this.

the reality that there are churches which do not exercise a biblical ministry is essential if effective mission to the nation is to take place. Such an acknowledgement is immensely painful but necessary.[141] The consequence of such an acknowledgement will then be the recognition that there are areas and communities in which no Christian witness is present (even after allowing for the presence of congregations from other denominations).

The acknowledgement that there are Church of England churches which no longer have a recognisably Christian witness and ministry need not be done in a public and accusatory manner. The problem of the holes in the parish system generated by this theological confusion can be addressed by two simple means. One is to exercise a theological discipline over those who are ordained and licensed to churches. Another is to adopt the recommendation made in the report *Mission-Shaped Church* that Church of England incumbents should not be able to veto the establishment of another congregation led by a licensed Anglican minister in 'their' parish territory.[142]

---

[141] The sensitivity of this issue can be gauged through the consultation conducted by the Toyne report which asked various bodies how desirable or essential it was that mission initiatives "should not undermine the virtues of the parochial system and should not threaten the different integrities within the church". See Toyne, *A Measure for Measures*, p 32.

[142] Cray, *Mission shaped Church*, p 149 has as its recommendation "the removal of the canonical right to exclude further Anglican churches, where their creation has been sanctioned by the bishop in line with procedures authorized by the new Pastoral Measure". On pp 141-2 this is alternatively stated in these terms: "Our suggestion is to request church legislation to change the canonical right to exclude the arrival of further Anglican churches whose creation has been sanctioned by the bishop in line with agreed diocesan procedures". The relevant Canon is C8.4. This is also implicit in Recommendation 18 (on Mission initiatives) made in Toyne, *A Measure for Measures*, since paragraph 3.31 states "While there should

The reality of social irrelevance /   ineffectiveness

Examples of churches and congregations that appear to be flourishing can mask the minimal impact that Christian mission is having upon this country.[143] While lively congregations in rural areas can still have a significant impact upon their community through the existing parochial system this is not the case in urban areas, which of course are precisely where the majority of people live in England. The problem is that Church of England Anglicanism lacks what Tim Dakin calls "the structure of self-extension".[144] By this he means that the structures and governance of the Church of England in this country are dominated by the territorial ideal. Dakin points out that the rise of voluntary societies in the nineteenth century to provide a means of self extension is a symptom of this state of affairs. Of course this does not mean that we have to abandon the best ideals of the parish system, but we must certainly rethink its expression today.

Pursuing the ideals of the parish system today

Historically Christian mission has been most effective when its structures and organisation have mirrored the networks of the society to which it is ministering. We can see this occurring during the Anglo-Saxon period with the identification of dioceses with the tribal kingdoms and the

---

be no right of veto on the part of the incumbent of a parish over an initiative..."
See Toyne, *A Measure for Measures*, pp 31, 34.
[143] See P.F. Jensen, *Christ's Gospel to the Nations, Latimer Briefing 5* (Latimer Trust, London: 2003) pp 24-28 for a brief and accessible survey of the evidence for the collapse of Christianity in Britain.
[144] T. Dakin, *Church Mission Societies: Scaffolding or Structure of the Spirit?, The JC Jones Memorial Lecture 2001* (Church Missionary Society, London: 2001) p 17.

later subdivision of those original dioceses as certain kingdoms such as Wessex grew and came to predominate. We can see it in the way that private, patronal churches centring on villages and estates came to be built during the late Anglo-Saxon period. Prior to the rigidity of the parish system which became established by the twelfth century there was a certain flexibility and variety which enabled the structures to adapt to the society to which the Church was ministering.

A similar conformity to social and political structures can be seen in the way the Anglican Communion developed to reflect the creation of the British Empire. At a smaller scale one can see the development of gilds during the medieval period as reflecting particular social networks. For centuries there have been chaplaincies through which Christian ministry has been provided to particular communities which have been defined by different social circumstances (army regiments, naval ships, hospitals, schools etc).

Mission-shaped Church is therefore correct in identifying the importance of networks in today's society.[145] The Church must go where people are. Today this will mean recognising the existence of ethnic groupings, the significance of places of work, the networks created through schools and so on. Although it is important to place a priority on regular congregation meetings that take place in areas where people actually live, these wider networks require that churches work together in the task of evangelism and discipleship. Lay leadership and training will be important for this. Even in rural areas where the nature of the communities still makes sense in relation to the parish system, the norm of

---

[145] Cray, *Mission-shaped Church*, pp 11-12.

the single minister being responsible for several churches requires the same development of lay ministry. Pursuing the ideals of effective mission and pastoral care today will also involve working with congregations of other denominations who have the same vision. This will need a renewed commitment to the proper Anglican ideal of mere Christianity and a determination to establish effective doctrinal discipline as well as to eschew denominationalism. Perhaps the pursuit of this vision over time will gradually recreate a national organisation of Christians that will genuinely deserve the title Church of England.

Working from within the Church of England for the ideals of the parish system

It is not easy for an organisation that has inverted biblical priorities concerning mission and structure to renew its vision for ministry work and mission. However the increasing awareness that the current system is in crisis gives the opportunity for certain key steps to be taken. I would suggest that priorities should be:

(i) A commitment to the consistent exercise of theological and moral discipline in those ordained and licensed to serve in the Church of England

(ii) A removal of the canonical right to exclude other Anglican churches from operating within a parish (even though fees continue to be directed towards the historic Anglican church in that parish)[146]

---

[146] As highlighted above (p 54), this is one specific recommendation in Cray, *Mission-shaped Church*, pp 142, 149.

(iii) A shift in attitude so as to view the Church of England parish as being the worshipping congregation when it is assessed for financial and other purposes (in other words a move away from defining the parish through the number and social characteristics of people living in its geographical boundaries). The organisation of the Church of England's finances should not reinforce the existing parish system and its territoriality, when there is no longer any necessity to do so.

Naturally (i) is the hardest challenge, but even if this is not taken up (ii) and (iii) would improve the possibility of more effective ministry and growth.

The minster model

Among those who acknowledge the nature of the crisis facing the Church of England it is common to hear the minster model advocated as a way forward. Just as with its historical usage (see above pp 11-18), this term remains very slippery. The concept as it is used in the Church today needs to be examined carefully.

The first point to be made is that if the minster model refers merely to the way outreach and pastoral care was organised in Anglo-Saxon England then it must be rejected. The reality is that a structure like that (despite its virtues of flexibility) is inappropriate for an urban society that is enormously remote from the rural society of that period. There is also a sense in which the 'minster model' as commonly understood today[147] was in fact practised in the large manufacturing districts of England during the

---

[147] See Spencer, *Parochial Vision*, pp 104-119.

nineteenth century. There were then many examples of parishes where a central church was the key resource for a host of workers (lay and ordained) who operated from a number of convenient meeting places such as mission halls and schoolrooms (which were licensed for worship). It did not prove to be the answer to effective urban mission.

The second point is that reference to 'the minster model' can signify a search for a structural solution to the Church of England's crisis in mission and ministry. This study has aimed to show that the desire for such a solution often betrays an unwillingness to place the gospel itself as the chief resource for the growth and strength of the Church of England. The health of the Church of England is dependent on a commitment to gospel ministry and not to a particular structure or order. This explains why evangelicals are often accused of having little notion of ecclesiology. An ecclesiology which makes the gospel its foundation and priority and allows for flexibility in organisation and structure will not be very attractive for those who are convinced that it is order rather than teaching which will keep the Christian community in good health and exercising effective ministry. John Venn had the right (and evangelical) ecclesiology when he said "I would sacrifice a great deal to preserve Church order, but not the salvation of souls".[148]

A final word

It is not difficult to find examples today where a refusal to acknowledge the biblical priority of mission over order leads

---

[148] M. Hennell, *John Venn and the Clapham Sect* (Lutterworth Press, London 1958) p 234. Quoted by Dakin, *Church Mission Societies: Scaffolding or Structure of the Spirit*, p 2.

to the parish system being given a prominence and position it should not have. A report in the *Vancouver Sun* describes the battle between two congregations of the Anglican Church in New Westminster (ACiNW) for the ownership of their buildings.[149] The Rev Ed Hird of St Simon's Church in Vancouver is struggling to establish ownership of the church building by the congregation over against the diocese and the position adopted by George Cadman, the chief legal officer of the diocese of New Westminster. The report states that the battle is actually over the meaning of the word 'parish': "Hird argues that people in his congregation make up the 'parish' and that they agreed as a group to disassociate from the Anglican Church of Canada. But Cadman and the diocese argue that a parish cannot leave the diocese, as it is the area served by the church". The logical consequence of the diocese's position is therefore that there is a parish even when there is no congregation in that parish. Transposed to this country and given a wider scale, that would imply that there would still be a Church of England even when it has no members, simply because a parish system with defined territorial boundaries exists.

If the parish system is not given its proper place as a servant of the mission of the Christian community, then one fears that this might indeed be the ultimate fate of the Anglican church in this country. Structures, organisation and order are important for the welfare of the Christian community but they must be given secondary place behind God and his mission in our world. The parish system has

---

[149] Article by Amy O'Brian in the *Vancouver Sun*, July 14 2004, (http://www.canada.com/vancouver/vancouversun/news/westcoastnews/story.html?id=3a31cbd7-be9f-4c23-9860-5f094b73af24&page=2, accessed 21 July 2004).

ideals of evangelism and pastoral care which should be recognised as entirely proper: nevertheless, those ideals cannot be made practically effective while a particular system that froze in the twelfth century is idolised.

Bibliography

Addleshaw, G.W.O. (1957) *The Early Parochial System and the Divine Office* (A.R. Mowbray for the Alcuin Club, London)

ARCIC (1982) *Final Report* (CTS/SPCK, London)

Atkinson, N. (1997) *Richard Hooker and The Authority of Scripture, Tradition and Reason: Reformed Theologian of the Church of England?* (Paternoster, Carlisle)

Avis, P. (1998) 'What is Anglicanism?', in S. Sykes, J. Booty, and J. Knight (eds) *The Study of Anglicanism* (SPCK, London) pp 459-476

Avis, P. (2000) *The Anglican Understanding of the Church: An Introduction* (SPCK, London)

Balleine, G.R. (1951) *A History of the Evangelical Party in the Church of England* (Church Book Room Press, London)

Bassett, S. (1992) 'Church and Diocese in the West Midlands: The Transition from British to Anglo-Saxon Control', in J. Blair and R. Sharpe (eds), *Pastoral Care before the Parish*, pp 13-40

Best, G.F.A. (1964) *Temporal Pillars: Queen Anne's Bounty, the Ecclesiastical Commissioners, and the Church of England* (Cambridge University Press, Cambridge)

Blair J. and Sharpe, R. (1992) 'Introduction' in J. Blair and R. Sharpe (eds), *Pastoral Care before the Parish* (Leicester University Press, Leicester) pp 1-10

Brown-Lawson, A. (1994) *John Wesley and the Anglican Evangelicals of the Eighteenth Century: : A Study in Cooperation and Separation With Special Reference to the Calvinistic Controversies* (Pentland, Edinburgh)

Burkill, M. (1999) *Lambeth 1998 - The Death of Anglicanism?*, Churchman 113 pp 30-47

Burns, A. (1999) *The Diocesan Revival in the Church of England c.1800-1870* (Oxford University Press, Oxford)

Clarke, B.F.L. (1963) *The Building of the Eighteenth-Century Church* (SPCK, London)

Cray, G. (2004) *Mission-shaped Church: Church Planting and Fresh Expressions of Church in a Changing Context* (Church House Publishing, London)

Dakin, T. (2001) *Church Mission Societies: Scaffolding or Structure of the Spirit?, The JC Jones Memorial Lecture 2001* (Church Missionary Society, London)

Dearing, J. (1993) *The Church That Would Not Die* (Baron Birch, Whittlebury)

Ecclestone G. (ed.) (1998) *The Parish Church?: Explorations in The Relationship of The Church and The World* (Mowbray, London)

Foot, S. (1992) 'Anglo-Saxon Minsters: A Review of Terminology', in J. Blair and R. Sharpe (eds), *Pastoral Care before the Parish*, pp 212-225

Frend, W.H.C. (1982) 'Romano-British Christianity and the West: Comparisons and Contrasts', in S.M. Pearce (ed.) *The Early Church in W. Britain and Ireland: Studies Presented to C.A. Ralegh Radford, Arising from a Conference Organised in his Honour by the Devon Archaeological Society and Exeter City Museum* (B.A.R., Oxford) pp 5-16

Green, S.E.A. (1975) *St James' Ryde* (Ffrancon Press, Ryde)

Hennell, M. (1958) *John Venn and the Clapham Sect* (Lutterworth Press, London)

Jacob, W.M. (1997) *The Making of the Anglican Church Worldwide* (SPCK, London)

Jenkins, T. (2003) 'Anglicanism: The only answer to Modernity', in D. Dormor, J. McDonald, and J. Caddick (eds) *Anglicanism: The Answer to Modernity* (Continuum, London) pp 186-205

Jensen, P.F. (2003) *Christ's Gospel to the Nations,* Latimer Briefing 5 (Latimer Trust, London: 2003)

Jones, A. (2000) *A Thousand Years of the English Parish: Medieval Patterns and Modern Interpretations* (Windrush Press, Moreton-in-Marsh)

Longham, M. (2001) *Buxton: A People's History* (Pentland Press, Lancaster)

Morgan, I. (1965) *The Godly Preachers of the Elizabethan Church* (Epworth Press, London:)

Norman, E.R. (2004) *Anglican Difficulties: A New Syllabus of Errors* (Morehouse, London)

Overton, J.H. (1894) *The English Church in the Nineteenth Century (1800-1833)* (Longmans, London)

Packer, J.I. (1991) *Among God's Giants: Aspects of Puritan Christianity* (Kingsway, Eastbourne)

Pytches, D. and Skinner, B. (1991) *New Wineskins: A Plea for Radical Rethinking in the Church of England to Enable Normal Church Growth to Take Effect Beyond Existing Parish Boundaries* (Eagle, Guildford)

Redfern, A. (2000) *Being Anglican* (Darton Longman & Todd, London)

Richardson, J.P. (1998) *'To Our Own People Only': Re-owning Original Anglicanism*, Churchman 112 pp 124-130

Ryle, J.C. (1883) *Can They be Brought in?* (Hunt & Co.: London)

Sachs, W.L. (1993) *The Transformation of Anglicanism: From State Church to Global Communion* (Cambridge University Press, Cambridge)

Sceats D. (1996) 'Orders and Officers of the Church', in I. Bunting (ed.) *Celebrating the Anglican Way*, pp 179-198

Scotland, N. (2004) *Evangelical Anglicans in a Revolutionary Age 1789-1901* (Paternoster, Carlisle)

Seaver, P.S. (1970) *The Puritan Lectureships: The Politics of Religious Dissent, 1560-1662* (Stanford University Press, Stanford CA)

Sharpe, R. (1992) 'Churches and Communities in Early Medieval Ireland: Towards a Pastoral Model', in J. Blair and R. Sharpe (eds), *Pastoral Care before the Parish*, pp 81-109

Spencer, N. (2004) *Parochial Vision: The Future of the English Parish* (Paternoster, Carlisle)

Stock, E. (1899) *The History of the Church Missionary Society Vol 1* (Church Missionary Society, London)

Sykes, S. (1996) 'The Anglican Character', in I. Bunting (ed.) *Celebrating the Anglican Way* (Hodder & Stoughton, London) pp 21-32

Thacker, A. (1992) 'Monks, Preaching and Pastoral Care in Early Anglo-Saxon England', in J. Blair and R. Sharpe (eds), *Pastoral Care before the Parish*, pp 137-170

Toyne, P. (2004) *A Measure for Measures: In Mission and Ministry* (Church House Publishing, London: 2004)

Wright, N.R. (1982) *Lincolnshire Towns and Industry 1700-1914* (History of Lincolnshire Committee for the Society for Lincolnshire History and Archaeology, Lincoln)